His Joy, My Strength: A collection of Poetry to encourage & uplift.

Ja'Braun Mckenzie

BookLeaf Publishing

Presentation by *BookLeaf Publishing*

Web: www.bookleafpub.com

E-mail: info@bookleafpub.com

ISBN: 9789357211123

First edition 2022

DEDICATION

I have a couple of dedications. Firstly, this book is again dedicated to the memory of my deceased father Master Sergent Darryl E. Mckenzie (9/11/57- 2-11-2002) without you I wouldn't be here today. Also, in loving memory to the most incredible grandmother a guy could have ever been blessed with Alma L. Barnfield 2/25/27-4/16/15. Lastly, but certainly not least my loving, dedicated, & hardworking Mother Debra Mckenzie , whom has been there for me every step of the way throughout all of my health challenges, failures, & successes. She is truly more than a mother; she is my confident & best friend.

ACKNOWLEDGEMENT

I would definitely like to acknowledge the book leaf group for giving me this awesome opportunity to share & release a piece of my heart with the world. It has indeed been a long time coming. I would also like to acknowledge my family for their constant love and support. My Mother Debra Mckenzie, Big Brother Jovan Mckenzie , Sister Janea Smith, & Brother Brandon Ross. My loving Aunt Pamela Moody & Uncle Chaz Moody for having a big hand in raising me. Also, to my Mentors & Pastors along the way Pastor Derrick Pd- Johnson (Jackie Johnson), Pastor Tim Steir (Krystal Steir) & my supportive few, but mighty friends Bianca Pattison, Qwatavia Michelle Hamilton, Molly Mims, Alfredo Moody & Alton White. Thank you all for being there for me throughout the years & even if we don't talk every day, I am so thankful to call you friends more like (Sisters & Brothers) many times. I love you all & to any one I may have forgotten charge it to my head & not my heart for sure. The list goes on & on.

PREFACE

This book has truly been birthed out of a long-time passion of crafting poetry & songwriting. It has been one of my biggest dreams & joys since before I even officially learned how to write. I have always written often to elevate my own mood through a battle with depression & anxiety as a result of growing up predominately in a single parent home & often having low self-esteem because I was teased for battling obesity & being socially awkward during adolescent years. This book speaks to all those issues, as I want readers to come away from this collection of 21 poems feeling truly empowered & realizing that the Joy that comes from heaven above truly is authentic & supersedes any earthly Joy.

Keep Smiling

I consider it a blessing, a unique gift that I possess. This ability I have to keep smiling in the midst of adversity and keep on moving even during those times when I may be in fact sad or feeling in distress. I know already what you may be thinking. I must mean putting on a facade and smiling unauthentically, but it is quite the opposite in all actuality. I am talking about a spirit of joy that is unshaken by my circumstances or surroundings. A smile that emanates from a place that is in fact not of this world that I wear proudly, because many times I thought it would be lost forever, but instead it comes back each time stronger than ever. His strength has sincerely been made perfect in my weakness. There's a saying that states it cost nothing to smile. I do agree with this to an extent, but I would also like to introduce this idea that says perhaps in fact it does cost the person that is smiling something because life sometimes does absolutely come to try to steal and crush our spirits and if we let it win it can succeed. It cost the price of letting go of every bad experience, disappointment, and memory & in its place filling it with the good ones that you want to have in the future, so yes, I smile although my inner being has at times felt utterly destroyed and way past broken. It is for me not a fake it 'till I make it mentality, but instead a bold & brave expression that says I may get weary at times, but I will never give up & allow the enemy to have my joy. I also know without sounding prideful or cocky at all that the smile on my face can potentially help someone else's day to be just a little bit brighter. Whether it be behind a mask or not I've been told that I even smile behind my eyes & I definitely know that it is the light of Christ that shines through me, and it is something that I certainly don't at all take lightly.

Fear Not

I'm letting them go, laying them aside all the fears I've held deep within. Casting them down every thought and imagination that has taken grip and played evil tricks on my mind. Those that say to me I can never live truly free or be everything my good, good father has called me to be. One's that say I might as well face it I will not succeed. I will no longer allow my own boundaries to limit my kingdom potential. I must flee from residing inside a cage that wasn't built for my hopes and ambitions to be constrained. The what if I don't, the maybe it wonts that have sheltered me from truly seeking out the endless stream of opportunities that are plentiful and boundless if only I would receive. I am now choosing with great intention to change the narrative and shift my perspective from crippling fear to unrelenting faith. The negative what if questions have now been replaced with confident decrees of it will come to pass, & I am more than a conqueror. I am more than a conqueror. I am rising and steadily renewing my mind daily one step at a time. Realizing more & more just how bright my light was meant to shine. Thou shalt not fear, fear not again I say

I've done that far too often already throughout my years. It's time to overcome & that I shall do just as I've always known somewhere in my subconscious thoughts that I was always born to do.

Mustard Seed Faith

I could choose to focus on all that is wrong in the world. Dwell on the suffrage, the hurt and the pain, or I can choose instead to move forward with mustard-seed faith. It may feel like all the anguish and grief are slowly zapping away my energy. Yet, I make a decision to refuse to let go of this grain, knowing that if I lose my faith, I'll lose everything. I've chosen to withstand the tide of times & go the distance. In my pursuit of His purpose, I'll be ever persistent. Christ is calling me to move forward and remain relentless. I've made a promise to myself that I won't grow weary in well- doing - for I know I'm going to reap in due season. The troubles of this world try to tear me down, but I can't lose my hope or grow weary. A tiny mustard seed is all I need, so don't dare count me out.

Appointed Time

God has a set time to bless, despite every dark cloud that's been trying to loom. Every rain cloud must pass over soon in order for flowers to flourish, grow, & to bloom. Although, this present moment may be a time in life where everything feels like nothing's changing at all. Rest assured that He understands the pain. Be anxious for nothing God's up to something, endure just a little while longer. Yes, frustration is real, but his love is even more real. He's our healer and at any given moment the windows of heaven will lift & the doors will fling wide open. They that sow in tears will reap in joy endure hardness as a good soldier and it will soon be over. Believe & remember that it will all come to pass at the appointed time. God will speak & he won't lie, He will change every facet & detail of your life. Stand still & know that he is God & God alone. He will fulfill every one of his promises. He knows the day, the time, & hour He does, He truly does. He has a set time to bless each of his children abundantly well.

Visionary

visionary: keep the vision ever before your face. Visionary focused you must remain. Write the vision and keep it in plain sight, so if ever you do take your eyes off the prize even for a moment, you will have it as a reference point to always quickly remind & get back on a steady path. Through every circumstance, in the midst of every challenge remain grateful and keep your trust firmly grounded in God knowing that he has a grand plan for our lives. Knowing & keeping this one fact alone in mind must help us to spur on further and continue to fight. Everyone has a purpose; everyone has a light that both needs & deserves to shine bright. We are visionaries, so let us walk as such and never allow ourselves to become brutalized and traumatized by our experiences and disappointments of the past.

Journal Through My Journey

Never questioned it, never gave it much thought. It was as much a part of me as the hand attached to wrist as natural as breathing was my connection to words penned to paper. It didn't have to find me; I didn't have to find it. We were drawn to each other magnetically, for as long as I can remember. That's how I knew it was forever meant to be one of the deepest parts of me. Therefore, this love has led me to Journal through my journey of life. It has been one that has not always seemed fair, not at all always been kind. Instead of complaining I choose to write to express my heart & the words that I could not otherwise seem to find to convey the emotions I could not adequately verbalize. The journal on my journey has been a key component to my survival, but God knew my reason for being long before my arrival. My words will help to set not only myself, but others free. This poetry to some may be a lost art form only relevant to a few eccentrics, yet for me it's therapy and on far more than one occasion it has helped to save my life. There is no way I could ever make it without this gift that has been so graciously bestowed upon me. I know now more than ever before it was not meant to be kept inside selfishly. All that has been locked away must now be unveiled. I have been created to uplift, Inspire, and Heal as my alliteration helps broken hearts & wounded spirit's repair. I've been in a fight, a purpose driven fight to share, so here it goes there's no more time left to spare. I have no idea where this journey will ultimately end up taking me, but if these words inspired by actual life events will help at least one lost and empty soul feel whole & find peace then I'll know my goal is accomplished and I am complete. I hope you'll come along with me.

Empowered

Empowered to prosper, called to conquer, endowed with anointing & spiritual gifts by the one who sent us into the earth. He has not given us over to death, but instead he has sanctified us through the blood of his Son & sent back the Holy Ghost to be our comforter. Now, we are adopted into the family of believers. Now we are Sons & Daughters, Kings & Queens. Royalty so we should stand up & take our rightful places knowing that we have been empowered to live with kingly authority. In a place of healing far from sickness and strife, far removed from the ailments of life when we stand with Dunamis power.
Empowered, we have been empowered to change the world and shake the nations. We have been called to fulfill his Holy Mandate. We have been empowered & we must busy ourselves by consistently being His hands upon his blessed soil. Remaining strong and of good courage, knowing that we are his citizens & earthly representatives. He is ours and we are His so why don't we stand up & act like it. We are His, He is ours. We've got the power. We have been empowered, sing Hallelujah we are

the Kings kids so why don't we act like it? Fore now is truly the time to stand up & act like it.

The Fire

Don't back away from the fire, don't step away from the flame. The fire wants to build you, the fire desires to shape. So, whatever you do don't back away. Although the heat is intensified know that its purpose is to refine. Never lose your praise, keep your head held high & you'll come out unscathed. Beloveds think it not strange while going through diverse trials know please know that it's only the trying of your faith & it works patience. Therefore, don't give up, don't back away. The fire wants to transform you. Don't back away no don't try to escape. You'll come out shiny & bright. You'll come out as pure gold. If & only if you stay, you'll come out the furnace just as Shadrach, such as Meshach, & just like Abednego. He's that all-consuming fire he'll speak to you just like he spoke to Moses in the burning bush so whatever you do don't back away.

Believe in Miracles ?

Do you believe in miracles? I surely do. You ask why? I will both gladly & boldly reply, because when you look at me you are looking one square in the eye. When I look back over my nearly three decades of life, I can attest to the numerous times in which I've had intervention from beyond the sky. Miracles are blessings that are meant for all. Miracles are ready & waiting for those who simply call. They can come in different forms, they come to set free at times when life appears to no longer seem like the norm. Miracles are God's way of letting us know that he is there, they help us to remain calm in times when it feels as if he is distant & we are in despair. Yes, they come when we may least expect & during periods of our deepest stress. After hearts have been torn, they can be performed to mend. They are often answers to persistent prayers. Are miracles still relevant for this world today? If you were to ask me, I'd have to say absolutely without one moment of hesitation. God manifest His glory to us in both new and countless ways each & every single solitary day. Jesus is both the same yesterday, today, & forever. He is ever worthy to be praised. Remember this always if you are in need of a miracle trust me for you if you are open, one is always available as long as you still have breath. It surely awaits if you're willing to put your doubts & pride aside. Prove Him now, put Him to the test. He's still performing miracles I assure you. Hello out there aren't you even the least bit convinced yet?

We Shall Overcome

Even through the wreckage & debris that remains. Through the floods & hurricanes, & the scars they may leave behind. We will not sit down and accept defeat. We will not buckle, will not bend. We will not bow down as we wait for relief instead. We will wave banners and shout victory. Tattered and torn, weathered and worn. although we may have been wounded in the process still, we are here to tell our stories and proclaim that hosanna reigns, & through the hurt & pain we will move past and one day at long last, I know we will overcome. Through the heartache and pain, trekking through the torrential rain still firm we will stand. We shall go in and possess the land. We know our lord will uphold us in the palm of his right hand, and I know for a fact that it shall come to pass at long last lo & behold we shall, we shall overcome.

Healing

Healing virtue flows from your spirit so divine. I know you ever so personally to be the healer of mine. You've mended not only the external which in plain sight can be seen, but also the internal scars, wounds, & everything in between. Jehovah Rapha you're my healer there is none like you, after these encounters, this experience with you I've found a love beyond comparison now no one else will do. Health is strength, Health is wealth, & you are the source of it all. Whenever I'm in need of healing you're the one I'll always cling to, the one I will forever call.

Home

Growing up felt all sorts of insecurities, felt so lost, abandoned and alone. Longing for a sense of belonging amidst a sea of uncertainty all the while in your presence was home. Suffered much loss, desperately seeking to win. Thinking if only I could attain a certain level of fame or monetary gain, some outward level of success, maybe then I'd truly be at peace & find rest. Never truly realizing all along that in your presence was truly home sweet home. There's an expression that states home is where the heart is, & although it sounds pleasant in my mind, I've often pondered it. Contemplating the validity after being displaced I can truly confirm this statement to be true. Home is not about four walls and a roof so much as it is a feeling of cozy that replaces the lonely knowing that God is always with me despite every feeling of unrest, and if he is for me than tell me who can ever be against. In him I find solace, I find my source of love, complete warmth, and confidence.

Not Enough Hours

Not enough hours in the day to show you how
much you truly mean to me, & if I had
ten-thousand tongue's it still wouldn't be enough
to sing praises to your name. You're so worthy
so much more worthy than I give you credit for
sometimes.

His strength , My Joy

The joy of the Lord my strength it is. Nehamiah said it best I couldn't have even dared to try to say it any better. I will stand by this profession both now, today, & forever. His strength is made perfect inside of my moments of weakness. I've witnessed this time over & time again firsthand in my life. I refuse to live my life as a broken record that replays the pain of my past over & over again. Instead, I've found in him a peace that does indeed surpass all understanding. There have been times I've experienced gut wrenching anxiety that I didn't think would ever subside. I thought that I would surely faint from the worry that I did ever so poorly try to hide. He has always been the rock that was higher than I. He has helped me to stand when I felt I would collapse under the pressure that I could no longer deny. Thank God for prayer, & His Holy word that have helped to be my guides. Also, this passion & catharsis provided by this gift he provided in the form of this poetry in which I write. His strength, my joy. In his presence I find sheer & pure delight. Without it I'd surely be a depressed messed & I wouldn't

know how to carry on without the comforter that
plays a major role in my day to day walk of life.

Glory Road

I don't want to live a life of the ordinary, or mundane. Do not want to live a life in which I simply merely just exist. Spending days that are wasted & time that is in vain. I want to wash the car, gas the tank & travel down glory road. I'm ready to rightfully claim my place as one of destiny's children forgetting all about the disappointments, setbacks, and previous failures that are behind me in my rearview mirror. I want to travel along my purpose driven path. I've come this far by faith, so at this point there's absolutely no need to slow down my pace. I got my hands on 10 &2 and my foot on the pedal, it's time to keep cruising towards life on another level.

Crashing

Today decided I'm not giving up. Today decided that I alone am more than enough. I am worthy to fight for myself & my dreams. Today full speed ahead. No more inhibitions and limitations, certainly no more fear despite the uncertainty. Destiny, into my destiny I'm crashing. Today no holding back, no more hesitation. Despite all my reservations. I was not born to live a life of complacency; I was created to succeed. I won't settle for mediocrity. I've had my share of adversities, but I'll let nothing stop me. Today is the day there's no time like the present. I'll live in the moment, I'll crash. Head on collision with my dreams.

Goodness

Goodness and mercy shall follow me all the days of my life. I am overwhelmed by your goodness. Overcome with emotion by your love. Oh, my goodness I can't believe all your goodness I have received you have blessed me in ways that I can't describe, yet it's so tangible can't be denied. How your blessings have been bestowed upon my life. There have been times in my life when all your goodness I truly didn't recognize. Now I see, I give you praise & glory for your grace & faithfulness. Hallelujah, at one time I was too blind to recognize that even though there's tragedy and even though there's pain in this world today. You are my melody, and the very reason I am even alive. I am covered, I am protected.

Sibling Rivalry

Sibling rivalry often gives way to the far greater, yet all-encompassing sibling loyalty. We may not always see eye to eye, yet we always go to bat for one another, & hate to see the other cry. Sibling rivalry we may fuss, argue, & fight but we will also willingly stand up & fight for each other without even thinking twice. Middle child syndrome they may say I was born in the middle of a headstrong older brother & younger sister, however after living in the midst of the chaos for so many years I don't think now that I would have it any other way. They call me the mediator, the levelheaded one being able to see things from an even perspective I guess you could say is the gift I was blessed with & the role I've come to play. Before little sister was born, I was the one who was the baby till that role gotten taken away. Even so I never felt as if I had been replaced. My world is filled with laughter that helps me to escape the pain & this is why I can gladly say sibling rivalry will always give way for sibling loyalty & I for one think that fact is far beyond great.

Thank God 4 U

I thank God for giving me you. The fact that he did is living proof of how much he loves me and is always & ever thinking of me. Lonely days were plenty instead of few, yet I refused to become bitter & give up on finding a love that was as real as could be from someone as beautiful & absolutely adorable as you. Thank God that I can hold you in my arms and look into your eyes and see the love that is now Yours, Mine, & Ours reflecting back at me. I feel it emanates as we embrace. See I have no doubt that we are on the same wavelength, completely in sync with a love that moves in unison. Lord, I pray that when they see us, they see one. Just as the father, Holy Spirit, & Son. You said a threefold cord is not easily broken at all; therefore, I know that with God at the center of it all our love will never fall. Together we can't fail. Our love can't help but prevail, see I'm the type of guy that doesn't easily trust, yet you broke every one of my walls down and have shown me what it really means to both love & be loved in return. It is a feeling that can only be described as divine and I know it is why each morning before you leave I kiss your cheek as

you sleep & silently whisper another prayer of
thanks for this immeasurable gift. I thank God
for you always. I'll never let a day go by without
acknowledging this great blessing in the form of
you that he did so graciously give.

Alma's Poem

G stands for grace, R is for rose your favorite flower also represents real which you always kept it with me. A is for Almighty, whom you always taught me to praise. N is for no one & I do mean absolutely no one can ever replace. D is for Dynamic as your vibrant personality & inner strength always was. M is for mature. The last A is for anointed Alma the Woman I was blessed to call mine. A grandmother is exactly as the name states a second mother which is grand, who's loving, compassionate and always understands. Even though mine has departed this life for the next I will always both now & forever feel fortunate & blessed, because God chose you to be mine. I will always remember the precious time spent with you & the vast wealth of knowledge that flowed from your heart. Your 88 years of life were not lived in vain. Your legacy will always live on & remain consistent through your kids & theirs for generations to come. We will always cherish & remember the warmth, spiritual wealth, & comfort which were found in Grandma's hands.

So Strong (Debra's Poem)

Taught me how to pray and always keep the faith. Showed me how to act when things don't go my way. Taught me how to hold my head up and keep moving on. No matter what this world throws my direction, you'll always have my back, and if I ever lost you of course I'd be sad, but I know that your legacy and your constant strength will live on through me. Always been so strong, always been so kind. Always look good & stay fly. Thank God I was blessed that He hand chose you to be my momma , so blessed I got you in my life. I think the world should have more phenomenal women & mothers like you. Ma You're my heartbeat , my homie & today I honor you publicly my incredible Nubian queen. Mamma you're so smart , you're so strong undoubtedly got it going on. Told me to dream big , taught me to always go for my dreams. When I wanted to give up you said no I don't think so , & now I'm here walking out & living in my destiny.

www.ingramcontent.com/pod-product-compliance
Lightning Source LLC
LaVergne TN
LVHW010949200726
843509LV00013B/2345